COOL
MAKERSPACE
GADGETS & GIZMOS

CONNECT IT!

CIRCUITS YOU CAN
SQUISH, BEND, AND TWIST

Elsie Olson

Checkerboard
Library

An Imprint of Abdo Publishing
abdopublishing.com

abdopublishing.com

Published by Abdo Publishing, a division of ABDO, PO Box 398166, Minneapolis, Minnesota 55439. Copyright © 2018 by Abdo Consulting Group, Inc. International copyrights reserved in all countries. No part of this book may be reproduced in any form without written permission from the publisher. Checkerboard Library™ is a trademark and logo of Abdo Publishing.

Printed in the United States of America, North Mankato, Minnesota
102017
012018

 THIS BOOK CONTAINS RECYCLED MATERIALS

Design: Sarah DeYoung, Mighty Media, Inc.
Production: Mighty Media, Inc.
Editor: Liz Salzmann
Cover Photographs: Mighty Media, Inc.; Shutterstock
Interior Photographs: iStockphoto; Mighty Media, Inc.; Shutterstock

The following manufacturers/names appearing in this book are trademarks: Duracell®, Elmer's® Glue-All™, Our Family®, Pyrex®, Squishy Circuits™, Target®

Publisher's Cataloging-in-Publication Data
Names: Olson, Elsie, author.
Title: Connect it! circuits you can squish, bend, and twist / by Elsie Olson.
Other titles: Circuits you can squish, bend, and twist
Description: Minneapolis, Minnesota : Abdo Publishing, 2018. | Series: Cool makerspace gadgets & gizmos | Includes online resources and index.
Identifiers: LCCN 2017944031 | ISBN 9781532112515 (lib.bdg.) | ISBN 9781614799931 (ebook)
Subjects: LCSH: Electronic circuits--Juvenile literature. | Creative ability in science--Juvenile literature. | Handicraft--Juvenile literature. | Makerspaces--Juvenile literature.
Classification: DDC 621.381--dc23
LC record available at https://lccn.loc.gov/2017944031

TO ADULT HELPERS

This is your chance to assist a young maker as they develop new skills, gain confidence, and make cool things! These activities are designed to help children create projects in makerspaces. Children may need more assistance for some activities than others. Be there to offer guidance when they need it. Encourage them to do as much as they can on their own. Be a cheerleader for their creativity.

Before getting started, remember to lay down ground rules for using tools and supplies and for cleaning up. There should always be adult supervision when using a hot or sharp tool.

SAFETY SYMBOL

Some projects in this book require the use of hot tools. That means you'll need some adult help for these projects. Determine whether you'll need help on a project by looking for this safety symbol.

HOT!
This project requires the use of a hot tool.

CONTENTS

What's a
MAKERSPACE?

Imagine a room buzzing with activity. All around you, budding **engineers** and happy crafters are creating amazing projects. Every tool or supply you can imagine is at the tips of your fingers. Welcome to a makerspace!

Makerspaces are areas where people come together to create. They are the perfect places to create cool projects using electrical circuits! These marvelous spaces are equipped with all kinds of materials and tools. But the most important tool is your imagination. Makers dream up brand-new circuit projects. They find ways to put new twists on existing circuit projects to make them their own. To do this, makers need to be problem-solving pros. Are you ready to become a maker?

BEFORE YOU GET STARTED

GET PERMISSION

Ask an adult for **permission** to use the makerspace and materials before starting any project.

BE RESPECTFUL

Share tools and supplies with other makers. When you're done with a tool, put it back so others can use it.

MAKE A PLAN

Read through the instructions and gather all your supplies ahead of time. Keep them organized as you create!

BE SAFE

Working with electricity can be **dangerous**, so stay smart! Keep your power source switched off when connecting wires. Prevent short circuits. Ask an adult for help when you need it.

WHAT IS A CIRCUIT?

A circuit is a closed loop that electricity can travel through. It needs a power source, such as a battery. It also needs a conductor, such as a wire. A circuit also has a load. This is a device that the circuit powers. A light bulb can be a load. A switch controls the flow of electricity. It breaks and connects the circuit so the flow can be turned off and on.

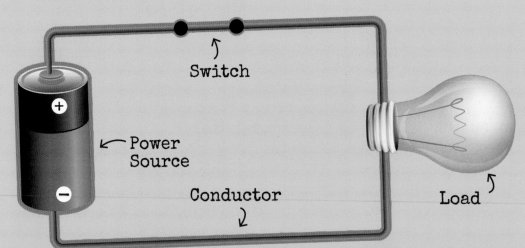

Switch

Power Source

Conductor

Load

SHORT CIRCUITS

Short circuits can happen when two conductors in a circuit touch that shouldn't. This can keep the electricity from reaching the load.

Short circuits can also be **dangerous**. They often cause wires and other metal parts to get very hot. They also drain the power source quickly.

DYNAMITE DOUGH

All the projects in this book use conductive and insulating dough. Conductive dough transports electricity. It allows you to easily connect circuit parts. The insulating dough does not conduct electricity. It can be used to separate pieces of conducting dough. It prevents short circuits!

Squishy Circuits is a company that sells conductive and insulating dough and circuit parts. The company's kits make building circuits easy!

You can also make your own dough. And you can buy circuit parts **online** or at hobby stores. Many parts can also be found in **robotics** kits.

SUPPLIES

Here are some of the materials and tools used for the projects in this book. If your makerspace doesn't have what you need, don't worry! Good makers are problem solvers. Find different supplies to substitute for the missing materials. Or modify the project to fit the supplies you have. Be creative!

aluminum foil

batteries

battery pack with terminals

buzzer with terminals

card stock

cookie sheet

craft glue

distilled water

electrical tape

food coloring

insulated copper wire

LED lights

measuring cups & spoons

motor with shaft

CONNECT IT! TECHNIQUES

pushpins

Styrofoam balls

vegetable oil

wire stripper

FUN FOR NOW!

Squishy circuits are made to be taken apart and rebuilt again. When the dough dries out, it loses some of its conductivity. It also damages wire and other metal parts. But conductive dough is a great way to practice building circuits. If a circuit works, you can look for a more permanent way to build it.

RED OR BLACK?

Batteries have negative and positive ends. Energy travels from the negative end toward the positive end. Because of this, many loads also have negative and positive connectors, such as wires. Positive is usually marked in red. Negative is marked in black. Use red and black wire and electrical tape when you are building a circuit. This helps you keep track of which parts are positive and which are negative.

CHOOSING A MOTOR

Motors with a lower **voltage** (5 volts or less) work best because they draw less electrical current. Motors from the Squishy Circuits kits work well for these projects. But you can also find motors **online** or at hobby stores.

CONDUCTIVE DOUGH

Make a sparkly dough that shimmers and shines as it conducts electricity.

WHAT YOU NEED

measuring cups

1½ cups flour, plus a few extra tablespoons

saucepan

¼ cup salt

measuring spoons

3 tablespoons cream of tartar

1 tablespoon vegetable oil

1 cup water

mixing spoon

food coloring

glitter

stove top

cookie sheet

plastic bag or airtight container

1. Put 1½ cups of flour in a saucepan. Add the salt, cream of tartar, vegetable oil, and water. Mix well.

2. Stir in food coloring and glitter until the mixture is the color you want it to be.

3. Cook over medium heat, stirring constantly until the mixture boils.

4. Keep stirring the mixture until it clumps together into a large ball.

5. Remove from heat. Allow the ball to cool for a few minutes.

6. Spread the remaining flour on a cookie sheet. Knead the flour into the ball. Stop when the dough is soft enough to shape but firm enough to hold the shape.

7. Store in a plastic bag or an airtight container.

TIP If you have a **gluten** allergy, you can use gluten-free flour.

INSULATING DOUGH

This sticky dough will stop electricity in its tracks!

1. Mix the sugar, vegetable oil, and 1½ cups flour together in a medium bowl.

2. Add the water, 1 tablespoon at a time, stirring constantly. Mix until the liquid is absorbed.

3. Stir in food coloring until the dough is the color you want it to be.

4. Put the dough on a cookie sheet. Knead a little of the remaining flour into the dough. Add more flour and knead it into the dough. Repeat until the dough is soft enough to shape but firm enough to hold the shape.

5. Store in a plastic bag or an airtight container.

 TIP Coat your hands with flour before kneading the dough. This helps keep the dough from sticking to your hand.

BLINKING DOUGH UFO

Create an out-of-this-world craft ready to light up the night.

1. Roll conductive dough into a ball about the size of a tennis ball. Flatten it into a disc. This will be your UFO base.

2. Roll insulating dough into a ball slightly smaller than a tennis ball. Flatten it into a disc.

3. Place the insulating dough disc on the conductive dough disc.

4. Roll another ball of conductive dough about the size of a tennis ball. Press the ball on the table to flatten one side. This is the top section of the UFO.

Continued on the next page.

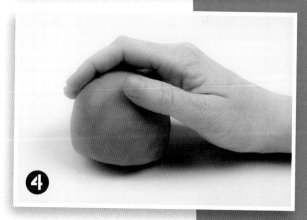

5 Place the top section on the insulating dough disc. Make sure no part of the top section touches the base.

6 Put the batteries in the battery pack. Push the positive **terminal** of the battery pack into the top section.

7. Push the negative terminal of the battery pack into the base.

8 Add an LED light. Push the positive (longer) LED wire into the top section. Push the negative (shorter) wire into the base.

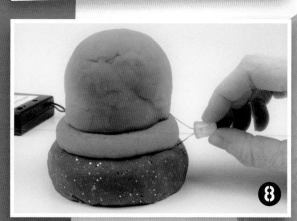

9 Repeat step 8 to add the remaining LED lights. Arrange them evenly around the UFO.

10. Test the lights. Turn on the battery pack. The lights should light up. If they don't, check that the LED wires are connected correctly.

11 Decorate your UFO! Use gems, craft foam, and more to make more lights and even an alien face!

TIP Modeling clay can replace insulating dough. Play-Doh can replace conductive dough. But it will not be as conductive as the dough made with the recipe on pages 10 and 11.

DISCO BALL IN A BOX

This gem-covered ball sparkles and shines as it spins around and around.

1. If the box has flaps, cut them off.

2. Cut a strip of card stock about 3 inches (8 cm) wide. It should be as long as the box is wide. Fold the strip in half the long way. Wrap the fold over one edge of the box. Glue it in place.

3. Cut five card stock pieces the exact size of the box sides. Use the card stock pieces to line the inside of the box. Glue one piece to each of the box's inner sides.

4. Cover your work surface with newspaper. Paint the Styrofoam ball and the outside of the box. Let the paint dry.

5. Glue gems all over the Styrofoam ball. Leave a small area uncovered. This will be the ball's top.

Continued on the next page.

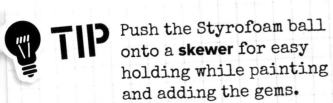

TIP Push the Styrofoam ball onto a **skewer** for easy holding while painting and adding the gems.

6. Set the box down. The edge with the card stock wrapped around it should be on the bottom. Use a pushpin to poke a hole in the middle of the top near the front.

7 Set the motor on the box with the shaft through the hole. Tape the motor in place.

8 Push the top of the Styrofoam ball onto the motor's shaft. Glue it in place if necessary.

9. Put the batteries in the battery pack. Tape the battery pack to the back of the box with the wires pointing up.

10 Form the conductive dough into two blocks. Set the blocks on the box. Make sure they do not touch each other.

II. Push the positive motor **terminal** into one block. Push the negative motor terminal into the other block.

12 Connect the battery. Push the positive battery terminal into the same block as the positive motor terminal. Push the negative battery terminal into the same block as the negative battery terminal.

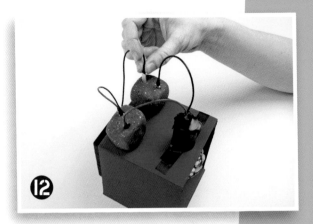

13 Decorate the box with stickers, glitter, and other materials.

14. Turn on the battery pack and watch your **disco ball** spin!

WHAT HAPPENS?

This project doesn't need insulating dough. The conducting dough blocks are separated from one another, so air acts as an insulator!

SPINNING OPTICAL ILLUSION WHEEL

Craft a mind-bending wheel that is sure to surprise once it starts spinning.

1. Set the plastic cup on a sheet of card stock. Trace around it. Set the cup aside.

2. Use a black marker to draw a **spiral**. Start in the center of the circle and go to the outer edge.

3. Use markers to color sections of the white space between the spiral's lines. Mix the colors slightly where they meet.

4. Cut out the wheel. Use a pushpin to poke a hole in the wheel's center.

Continued on the next page.

 TIP When you're designing a new circuit, draw it before building it. Know where all the wires will go. Label the positive and negative parts.

5 Roll two balls of conductive dough. Make them each slightly larger than a golf ball.

6. Flatten the balls into discs about 1 inch (2.5 cm) tall.

7 Roll a ball of insulating dough about the size of a golf ball. Flatten it into a disc about ½ inch (1.3 cm) tall.

8 Place the paper cup upside down on top of a conductive dough disc. Use the knife to cut the dough around the outside of the cup. Remove the cup. You should now have a dough circle.

9. Repeat step 8 with the other disc of conductive dough and the disc of insulating dough.

10. Place the insulating dough circle between the conductive dough circles.

11 Cover the outside of the motor with dough. It can be conductive or insulating dough. Do not cover the area around the shaft.

12 Press the motor onto the top circle with the shaft pointing up. Use additional dough to hold it in place if needed. Stick the positive motor **terminal** into the top circle. Stick the negative motor terminal into the bottom circle.

13. Put the batteries in the battery pack. Stick the positive battery terminal into the top circle. Stick the negative terminal into the bottom circle.

14 Push the wheel's hole onto the motor's shaft. Turn on the battery pack and watch your wheel spin!

15. Make more wheels with different patterns. Test them to see which one creates the best **optical illusion**!

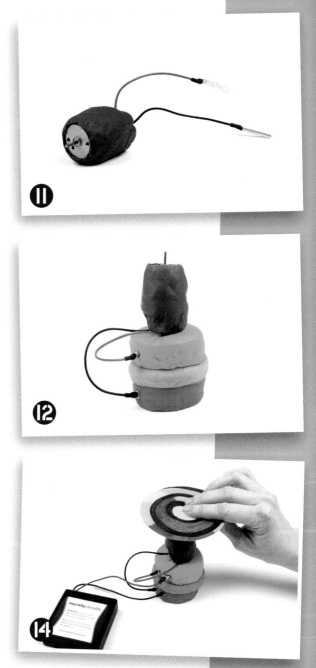

SQUISHY JOURNAL ALARM

No little brothers allowed! This noisy alarm will keep prying eyes off your secret stuff.

WHAT YOU NEED

red & black insulated copper wire

ruler • wire stripper

aluminum foil

conductive dough
(see pages 10 & 11)

battery pack with terminals

batteries for the battery pack

buzzer with terminals

red & black electrical tape

LED light • hardcover journal

clear tape

PRIVATE KEEP OUT

1. Cut three pieces each of red and black wire. Make each piece about 12 inches (30 cm) long.

2. Strip about 1 inch (2.5 cm) off both ends of each wire.

3. Tear off two pieces of foil. Fold each one into a 2-inch (5 cm) square.

4. Form six blocks of conductive dough. Put the batteries in the battery pack. Arrange the blocks, battery pack, buzzer, and foil squares like the **diagram** on page 29. Then follow the diagram and steps 5 through 11 to connect the wires.

5. Push the positive battery **terminal** into block 1. Push the negative battery terminal into block 2.

6. Twist one end of two red wires together. Push the free end of one wire into block 1. Push the twisted ends into block 3. Tape the remaining free end to a foil square. Use red electrical tape.

Continued on the next page.

7. Twist one end of two black wires together. Push the free end of one wire into block 2. Push the twisted ends into block 4. Tape the remaining free end to the other foil square. Use black electrical tape.

8 Push the positive buzzer **terminal** into block 5. Push the negative buzzer terminal into block 6.

9. Push one end of the unused red wire into block 3. Push the other end into block 5.

10 Push one end of the unused black wire into block 4. Push the other end into block 6.

11. Tape the positive (longer) LED wire to the foil square with the red wire. Use red electrical tape.

12 Place the foil and positive LED wire between two pages of the journal. The LED should be outside the journal with the negative (shorter) wire on top of the first page. Tape the foil in place with clear tape.

13 Tape the negative foil square inside the journal's cover with clear tape. When you close the journal, the foil should touch the negative LED wire.

14. Close the journal. Turn on the battery pack. The LED should light up. This means your alarm is set! If the LED does not light up, check your connections.

15. Open the journal. The buzzer should go off! If it does not, check your connections.

13

CIRCUIT DIAGRAM

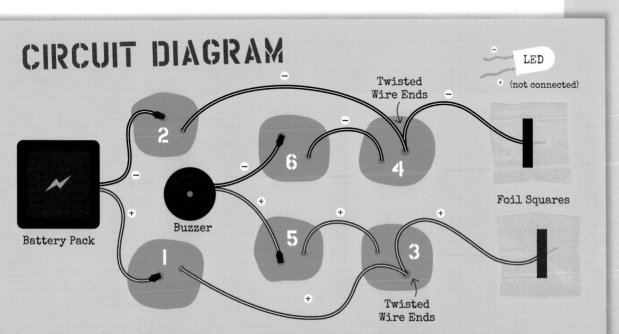

Twisted Wire Ends

LED

(not connected)

Battery Pack

Buzzer

Foil Squares

Twisted Wire Ends

MAKERSPACE MAINTENANCE

Being a maker is not just about the finished craft. It's about communicating and **collaborating** with others as you create. The best makers also learn from their creations. They think of ways to improve them next time.

CLEANING UP

When you're done with a project, be sure to tidy up your area. Put away tools and supplies. Make sure they are organized so others can find them easily.

SAFE STORAGE

Sometimes you won't finish a project in one makerspace **session**. That's OK! Just find a safe place to store your project until you can work on it again.

MAKER FOR LIFE!

Maker project possibilities are endless. Get inspired by the materials in your makerspace. Invite new makers to your space. Check out what other makers are creating. Never stop making!

GLOSSARY

collaborate – to work with another person or group in order to do something or reach a goal.

dangerous – able or likely to cause harm or injury.

diagram – a drawing that shows how something works or how parts go together.

disco ball – a shiny ball that spins and reflects light around a dance floor.

engineer – someone who is trained to design and build structures such as machines, cars, or roads.

gluten – a protein found in many grains, such as wheat and barley.

online – connected to the Internet.

optical illusion – something that looks different from what it actually is.

permission – when a person in charge says it's okay to do something.

robotics – the science of designing, constructing, and operating robots.

session – a period of time used for a specific purpose or activity.

skewer – a long, pointed stick.

spiral – a pattern that winds in a circle.

terminal – a device attached to the end of a wire or to electrical equipment for making connections.

voltage – electric force measured in volts.

ONLINE RESOURCES

Booklinks
NONFICTION
NETWORK
FREE! ONLINE NONFICTION RESOURCES

To learn more about circuit projects, visit **abdobooklinks.com**. These links are routinely monitored and updated to provide the most current information available.

INDEX